THE
BULLETIN

The Legacy of
Benny Goodlow

Jerald D. Johnson

Beacon Hill Press of Kansas City
Kansas City, Missouri

Copyright 1997
by Beacon Hill Press of Kansas City

ISBN 083-411-6731

Printed in the
United States of America

Cover Design: Mike Walsh
Cover Photo: Tony Stone Images

All Scripture quotations are from the King James Version.

10   9   8   7   6   5   4   3   2   1

CONTENTS

Dr. Jerald D. Johnson
General Superintendent
Emeritus, Church of the Nazarene

Dr. Larry C. Lott
Pastor, Blue Hills Church of the
Nazarene, Kansas City, Missouri

Introduction

I don't remember when Mr. Benny Goodlow and his family first arrived in our Nebraska town of about 5,000 people. At the time there were probably no more than 10 or 12 African-Americans in the whole county. As a boy of nine, it seemed to me they had always been a much loved part of our church. If anyone ever referred to them as "Colored," it was only because the Goodlows did so themselves. It made no difference to anyone. In the church my father pastored, we were all one close-knit family, loving and watching out for each other in the tough depression years. I often think of those times and the wonderful contribution Benny Goodlow made to all of our lives with his delightful *Bulletin*.

Recently I have been able to retrieve some copies of Benny's *Bulletin;* and as I read them again, their news of the times, their picture of small-town church life, and the wisdom of Benny's thoughtful editorials seemed worthy of a wider audience.

As I present them to you, I trust that the wisdom, insight, and homespun humor of this good man, Mr. Benny Goodlow, will bless and inspire you as it did us in those austere years of the Great Depression.

Since my recent years have been spent working out of the International Headquarters of the Church of the Nazarene, I felt it would be fitting for the royalties from this little book to go to the Church of the Nazarene nearest to where I work. This church is the Blue Hills Community Church of the Nazarene, served by the outstanding ministry of Dr. Larry Lott and his capable staff.

Under Dr. Lott's leadership the Blue Hills Community Church has outgrown its facilities and needs to expand.

This little book, therefore, is lovingly dedicated to Dr. Larry Lott. All proceeds from the sale of Mr. Benny Goodlow's story will be channeled to Blue Hills Community Church of the Nazarene in Kansas City. I trust that the story of Benny's *Bulletin* will offer courage and faith to Dr. Lott and his congregation as they face the challenge of broadening their capacity for service to their community. May the income from this book provide the seed money from which will come ample funds for the church to expand or move to larger facilities, whichever they choose to do.

—JERALD D. JOHNSON
General Superintendent
Church of the Nazarene

THE BULLETIN

The Legacy of Benny Goodlow

1

The Goodlows

NO ONE IN OUR SMALL TOWN OF 5,000 seems to recall when the Goodlows first came. It seemed as though they had always been there. As a boy of 8 or 9, I knew Mr. Benny Goodlow and his mother and sisters as much loved members of the church my father pastored, and warm personal friends of our family.

Mr. Benny Goodlow had fought in World War I. He was justly proud of this fact and talked of his battle experiences freely, to the enjoyment of the young boys in the church. He was one of our heroes.

Benny's mother was just that, a mother. Her children cared for her tenderly and lovingly, as she did them. As long as she lived, family activity always pivoted around her.

Benny had two sisters, Lily and Katy. Lily was happy, gregarious, and jovial. She was a born storyteller, and children gathered around her wherever she was, listening for one of her wonderful tales. Lily told one story that, as a boy, I thought was the greatest and the funniest of all. It happened in a church she attended before coming to our town. A mouse, she said, ran across the floor during the service. It stopped in front of her foot, then climbed aboard her shoe and, in a wink, scrambled up her leg as far as her thigh. At that point Lily grabbed her dress, squeezed for all she was worth, and began to scream. She got so excited she jumped up and down—all the while holding the trapped mouse and screaming in panic.

The congregation was unaware of the reason for her demonstration. They thought she was being blessed and shouting the praises of God. They all joined in, and everyone was soon a part of this "spiritual demonstration." Lily said she sneaked out of the church into the foyer and shook her dress. The mouse fell to the floor dead.

This was a great story to hear then, and we children demanded it many times. She left nothing to the imagination, and we relived it with her.

Where Katy was in the family, agewise, I don't recall anyone ever knowing. She was quieter than Benny or Lily and a bit more sophisticated. She was one of the most loving persons I have ever known. Katy was one of my mother's special and most intimate friends. Our entire family shared her affection for Katy.

Benny Goodlow was small in stature but sturdily built. To a large degree self-educated, Benny had a gift for words and a delightful sense of humor. He was everyone's friend—from the oldest granny in the church to the youngest boy. He was employed in a local hotel as dishwasher—a position envied by many in those depression years, when steady employment of any kind was a treasure. Benny was hardworking, dependable, and probably the best dishwasher that hotel ever had. Later, as a teenager, I worked in that same hotel. I found that Benny Goodlow was a legend among his fellow employees long after he was gone.

Benny Goodlow had a dream. He wanted to be a professional writer and editor. Today he probably would have achieved his goal. In those years it was an elusive dream for him, as it would have been for many others.

Yet, Benny did succeed, and the story of that success deserves to be shared. He did become a writer and editor. His church audience could hardly wait from one week to the next for succeeding editions of his paper. Many of his productions have been preserved and can now be shared with a new generation.

To appreciate what Benny Goodlow achieved, one must know something of the setting and of his audience. The Great Depression of the '30s was in full swing. Unemployment was very high, and when anyone secured a regular job, all of us rejoiced. A spirit of community helped us to survive. This friend-helping-friend mentality identified our small church fellowship of believers. A lack of money forced everyone—especially the youth group of the church—to be creative in finding meaningful things to do together.

In those years we were all alike in our church. There was little money, a lot of unemployment, and a spirit of sharing to help each other make it until a better day came. The memories of those days are precious. What stands out in my recollection are the good times we enjoyed in spite of how little we had.

With what little money Benny Goodlow earned at his dishwashing job (and it must have been very little) he not only supported his mother and two sisters but also budgeted for paper, carbon paper, and typewriter ribbons to put out his weekly *Bulletin.* He distributed it free of charge to the church family.

2

Benny Goodlow —
Editor, Publisher, Printer

BENNY GOODLOW TOOK SERIOUSLY his self-imposed task of editing and printing the *Bulletin*. He looked upon the weekly publication as his contribution to a rather small church family. The congregation of about 100 people experienced a unique bonding with one another through their shared interest in their own weekly newspaper.

Receiving Benny Goodlow's weekly *Bulletin* was one of the happy highlights in our small church. On Tuesday nights everyone wanted to be in prayer meeting at the church, for after the service the *Bulletin* would be distributed by the editor himself. Clusters of people would gather in the corners of the little white, frame building reading, chattering, and laughing. No one went home until the entire *Bulletin* was read. No editor or writer anywhere ever enjoyed the acclaim from their reading constituency more than Benny did on those Tuesday evenings.

Benny took great delight in reporting on budding romances. He would have made a great gossip columnist in any daily newspaper. It was the *Bulletin* that kept all of us abreast of the latest in our little "society." The *Bulletin* was a bit of happiness and cheer in the midst of what was otherwise a difficult time for many people. The *Bulletin* provided not only spice for our lives but encouragement to our faith as well.

Benny had names for nearly everyone. My father was the "Shepherd," and my mother, the "Shepherdess." He seemed to take great delight in writing about them, as he did with many others. He handled church news with aplomb, taking pleasure when he thought he sensed a new couple getting together. He received letters to the editor and responded to them. People in the church tried to hide their identity by using fictitious names in their letters to him. He kept these same people reading by trying to reveal who they were, in the next edition of the *Bulletin*.

Benny Goodlow must have spent all his free moments on his beloved *Bulletin*. He taught himself to type with two fingers. No one knows how many hours he spent making sure that the 17-23 typewritten pages were published on time. Carbon paper made it possible to make a few duplicates at once; but to have enough for all his readers, Benny had to retype an entire edition several times. In addition, he was his own publisher, distributor, and roving reporter. As a result of his commitment, today we have documentation of life in the '30s as experienced by a unique and wonderful group of people—the members and friends of the York, Nebraska, Church of the Nazarene, where my father was pastor.

3

The Bulletin

BENNY GOODLOW NAMED HIS WEEKLY PAPER *Bulletin, Story Book*. The people of the church referred to it simply as the *Bulletin*. He followed publishing procedures by dating and numbering all issues, and he typed across the top of each paper a scripture verse that obviously was his guiding principle for the *Bulletin*. After the date and the issue number were always these words: "'Let all things be done decently and in order.'—St. Paul" (1 Cor. 14:40). To Benny this seems to have meant that there would be nothing divisive, unkind, or critical written in his weekly newspaper. To all appearances, he never deviated from his purpose to print everything "decently and in order."

Following his stated principle there was always an editorial, headed by a scripture reference. Benny had deep spiritual insights. His writings on biblical and church themes reflect a timeless understanding and continue to have strong practical application today. He had a way of discerning the mood of the people and writing to uplift and teach. Who can know the number of discouraged members in those tough days who were encouraged to "keep holding on" by Benny's editorial "Sunshine"?

Sunshine

Matthew 9:37: "Then saith he unto his disciples, The harvest truly is plenteous, but the labourers are few."

It is not the Christian's lot to go about with a sad and gloomy and woebegone countenance. For a Christian to assume such an attitude is to advertise Christianity as a failure. Anything, no matter what it may be, that produces nothing but discouragement

16

and woe and misery is a failure—and a rank failure. Woe and misery and despair and wretchedness and discouragement, and all of the things which follow in the wake of these evils, are produced by sin and iniquity. All things in this world that tend to fret and vex and harry and worry the soul and mind of man are the direct agents of sin, under the control of Satan. Happiness is the Christian's lot, and happiness comes from God. Sin, no matter how beautiful it may seem, for sin often guises its self in beauty even as Satan often appears as an angel of light, cannot bring forth happiness. Men and women indulge in wild dissipations and immoralities and imagine that they are tasting of the fair fruits of happiness, but they are merely deceiving themselves. Happiness is not to be found along the highways of sin. The fruit which the deceived ones eat, thinking it to be the fair fruits of true happiness, turns to ashes in their mouths. There is neither rest nor happiness to those who seek rest and happiness in disobedience.

But those who love God and our precious Saviour, and strive to walk uprightly in the light which has been given to them, gain peace and happiness, and their lives, in spite of the trials and tribulations which must come in this world, should be lives of sunshine. They should always be cheery and optimistic, never sad, woebegone, and discouraged. The discouraged Christian, if such a one exists, is a pitiful object indeed. Why succumb to despair after you have reposed your faith in Him? Why fear and doubt after you have put your trust in Him?

Discouragement is the assassin of Faith. Discouragement is Public Enemy No. 1 to your soul, a criminal and an outlaw, whose only purpose is to tear down and destroy and kill. Get rid of him. Slay him. Show him no mercy. No Christian can afford to tolerate him for a moment. Fill the heart with sunshine and mirth and joy and optimism. These are the traits which belong to the Christian character.

If you have troubles, as many of us do, real troubles, take them to Jesus in secret and tell Him about them, and do not parade them before your friends, seeking their sympathy. Human sympathy does not solve problems. There are troubles that your best friends cannot handle. But Jesus can. Go to Him. And smile. Have sunshine in your attitude. Return a cheery answer. Laugh. It isn't a sin to laugh. Wear your sense of humor. A sense of humor, used rightly, is a great help. Sprinkle sunshine wherever you go. Stifle the gloom. Discard the long face. Forget that tale of woe. Have a testimony of hope and faith and gladness!

Following the editorials came the fun news. Benny seemed to enjoy writing about people and their lives. In one issue he called the pastor "the Shepherd" as usual, and then spoke of his wife as "the Shepherdress." Was the misspelling on purpose? Was it a subtle reference to the time when he received his World War I bonus and gave my mother money to purchase a beautiful new dress—an undreamed-of luxury in those days, and a gift she wore and enjoyed for many years?

One of the church families lived in the country. The *Bulletin* makes frequent reference to activities at their place, referring to it as the "Home on the Range." The farmer's wife was referred to as "the woman of cream separator fame."

Many people in the church, especially the ladies, enjoyed visiting in one another's homes quite frequently. Benny often wrote, tongue in cheek, about the "gadabouts" and their activities. Various copies of the *Bulletin* reveal Benny chiding, teasing, and generally having great fun writing of their doings. He gave these ladies of the church their own special names, letting the readers guess their true identities. One lady named Bessie was called Bessie

Bo-Peep. Then there were Ducky, Princess, Lady Placid, Blondie, and many others.

These references and news items would prompt letters to the editor. Benny thrived on this sort of response from his readers. He never failed to quote anyone who wrote to him. Someone in the church, identified as Johnny the Poet, responded to what Benny had been writing about the gad-abouts with a delightful bit of verse that Benny happily published:

> *Give me the life of a gadabout,*
>   *For I want to ramble and roam.*
> *I want to rise with the brightening sun*
>   *And flitter away from home.*
> *I want to go where I want to go*
>   *With no one to say me nay.*
> *I want to rove over hill and dell*
>   *And be happy and free and gay.*
> *I want to call on my neighbors and friends*
>   *And laugh and chat and dine.*
> *Oh the life of a gadabout is what I want,*
>   *So full and free and fine.*
> *I couldn't be a stay-at-home*
>   *From dawn unto the night.*
> *It would rob me of my sense of joy*
>   *And leave me in a plight.*
> *I couldn't stay home and brew and bake*
>   *And scrub the kitchen floor.*
> *I couldn't stay home to wash and iron*
>   *And do the common chore.*
> *For I must rove and ramble and roam*
>   *And call on my friends galore*
> *Who greet me with the smiles I love*
>   *When I tap upon their door.*
> *They invite me in, and their tea I drink*
>   *And I nibble their tasty food*

> *And we chat about the church and folk*
> > *And all this is very good.*
> *Oh give me the life of a gadabout,*
> > *For I want to ramble and roam.*
> *I want to rise with the brightening sun*
> > *And flitter away from home.*

Surrounding these lines in the *Bulletin* are Benny's cartoons. The drawings are simple and plain, but they say it all. Numerous paragraphs reveal that Benny was often in a quandary trying to figure out who had written such material to the paper under a fictitious name.

Sports articles also had their place in the *Bulletin*. Benny Goodlow loved softball and always was chosen to be the umpire in the games. These events were highlighted, reflecting keen but friendly competition. He liked the games of lawn croquet and horseshoes. The city park had grounds laid out for both these activities for public use, and church social affairs in the park always found Benny and a few others gathered where these games were played. Reading his reports of such competitions brings a keen sense of nostalgia for the simple pleasures of those days.

A trip to the city park by the people of the church for an outing planned especially for children displays the style and penchant of the editor to make the most of what today might be interpreted as nothing of importance at all. In a September 1935 issue Benny wrote:

> You've read Louisa May Alcott's *Little Men*, haven't you? Well, this story is nowhere as good as that, but it's a story anyhow. It concerns Saturday afternoon in Harrison Park.
>
> At that time the little men of our group picnicked under the careful and motherly sponsorship of the Nazarene Ladies Bible Class. Just Wednesday past the little women were highly entertained in a similar manner, and it was thought unfair to neglect the little men. So they had their outdoor party, and

even the fact that there were two little girls present did not deter them. They went right ahead and did their boy things in truly boy style.

And they were such fine little men and conducted themselves so obediently that the sponsors are still talking about them. Indeed, Mother Flynn declared repeatedly she had the best time at that picnic she has had in many a long moon, and it was mostly because the little men were really little men.

The little men's picnic was all over and they had gone home, but it was still too early for their sponsors to leave. They departed to the croquet court and staged the second heavyweight croquet battle of the year. The participants were The Matron, Countess Ruth, The Mayor of Frogville, Lady Placid, and Kay. The official scorekeeper—so far unidentified by the *Bulletin*—records that all three matches were won by The Matron, who is suspected of being a professional posing as an amateur. But the losers lodged no complaint with the *Bulletin* commission, so The Matron's victories shall be allowed to stand.

Lady Placid featured the game by stopping to giggle every time she made a nice shot. At the end of the match play Kay and The Mayor were so far in arrears that they decided the only way to catch up was to quit, which they did. Countess Ruth's play was good at times, and she was doubtless the next best player to the champion. Kay admits that she was the poorest player, but we do not believe that playing ability accounted for much in those games. It is said that preceding the croquet match Kay and Lady Placid pitched horseshoes, but we do not believe it was anything to write home to the folks about. But everyone had a joyous time, and they want to go back again.

That Benny Goodlow could find enough excitement in the lives of a few people in a small Midwestern town to fill 17 to 23 pages is amazing. Is it any wonder that those who are still alive from those days remember the happy times and somehow have been able to forget the hardships of that era? Without question, Benny Goodlow contributed greatly to those memories, enriching them with his prolific and imaginative writing.

In one issue written prior to the annual church picnic, Benny wrote: "Let's have the best church picnic on record —our record!"

One of those picnics prompted the editor to write:

Off to the park for a holiday with weenies and so on and the old croquet set. A bright sun shining warmly and summer lingering in the breezes. Wonderful day. Wonderful idea. Wonderful folks.

There was the slender wife of Edward Williams and the family Ponti. There was Lady Placid of the famous wearing apparel emporium. There was Ethel Neff, well-known nurse and seamstress, and there was Kay, the light heavy-weight gadding champion of our group. Quite a bunch of fours indeed to descend so suddenly upon caretaker Thompson, demanding croquet clubs and balls. But we suppose he is used to many extraordinary things.

It is said that a mere man joined himself to the party, and it is even said that he played croquet astonishingly well with them. And it is further alleged that he got in on the eats too. And if all this is true, he is about the only man who has shown enough courage to take part in one of these all-feminine croquet tournaments.

The royal eats consisted of weenies, toasted marshmallows, buns, pickles, and coffee, and it was quite good enough for Lindbergh, the Prince of Wales, or Madam McGreggor. As for the victories, Lady Placid playing with the honorable Jake, the man who butted in, defeated Mrs. Ed Williams and Mrs. Kay Robnett in the doubles. But later they played singles, and Mrs. Edward Williams walked off easily with the prize, which was probably the fattest weenie.

What puzzles this department though is this: Who took care of the Neff and Page Emporium while they were gadding about at the weenie roast?

(The Neff and Page Emporium was a used clothing store. The "family Ponti" referred to earlier was Ed Williams's Pontiac, and "Jake" was a recent German immigrant who eventually married Miss Page of the Emporium.)

The used clothing store was evidently a welcome business in town. An issue of the *Bulletin* endorsed it, saying, "The reporter [Benny himself] has discovered a fine new clothing store located at 417 Grant Avenue. *Bulletin* folks had better sit up and take notice. Just go down and find who you will see in charge."

Even a group of church folk getting together to work on a jigsaw puzzle was an event worth recording in the *Bulletin.*

> We haven't heard from the expert jig sawyers since Thanksgiving Day, but as no news is reputed good news, we suppose that they are still in pretty fair physical shape after their five-hour battle of last Thursday afternoon. That battle should go down in history as one of the decisive engagements of the age, as those grim gals fought against hunger in their determined efforts to crown their work with triumph; for repeatedly they were implored to quit their jiggy struggles and spread the table for the evening repast, but just as repeatedly they refused to quit the fight to partake of food, although they were hungry, which refusal indicates the great power of their endurance and patience!

Benny obviously wrote to be humorous to his readers. But, apparently, just in case there was not enough humor in his paper, he would use as fillers some jokes that were making the rounds in those days. Here are just a few:

Traveling Salesman: "May I show you my samples, sir? If you remember, I executed your last order with promptness and dispatch."
Important Person: "I gave you no order!"
Traveling Salesman: "Remember, sir, you said, 'Get out,' and I got."

* * *

"What do you mean when you refer to some person as a lemon?"
"I mean that he has a sour disposition and a yellow streak."

* * *

Chief Accountant: "There is two dollars missing from the cash drawer, and only you and I have a key to it."
Cashier: "Well, let's each put a dollar back and forget about it."

* * *

Sophomore: "These professors don't know a thing! Why, not one of them could teach and get away with it anywhere else. They are just dumb! They ought to get a whole new teaching staff."
Junior: "Yes, I flunked too."

* * *

Only humor could offset the frustrations of trying to keep an automobile running during the depression years. Benny wrote about one young man's car, which he called the "Spankit."

Of all the motor cars which Old King Kop has owned, we believe that the Spankit is the most celebrated. By that statement we do not mean to infer that the Spankit is the best car that he has ever owned—we believe he has owned better cars, even faster cars—but we do believe that the Spankit has made more real history and has played a greater part in that young man's existence than any of the several vehicles that have gone before.

The first car we have any distinct remembrance of is the one he drove to the State [district] assembly, the one which Duke used for headquarters, he and his sax. It was a noble old car and accomplished a lot of good, and we hated it when the King traded her off. Since that time we have become acquainted with Napoleon Pullapart and Caesar the Green Flash, both of which served the King well, and each played a prominent role in his many non-stop flights between Greenwood and East Hill (his home and that of his fiancee); but even at that there were times when Caesar would balk and refuse to function, times even when he would complain bitterly of flat tires; and as for Napoleon, he was even worse when it came to balking. Many grievous complaints were lodged against Napoleon. It is said that Nappy, by his nonsensical and uncalled for balking, nearly broke his young master's heart. But even with their eccentric ways, Nappy and Caesar managed to do fairly well between Greenwood and East Hill, with an occasional detour to the Country Club grounds.

But still we maintain that none of these cars attained to the heights now occupied by the Spankit. The Spankit not only took up where the others left off, but has done more. He not only entered into the non-stop endurance flights between Greenwood and East Hill with a stout heart and a willing engine, but he gave excellent service as well, and so far as we can learn, he has not been guilty of any grievous balking.

But yet we have not told you why the Spankit has become a celebrity among motor cars. But it is not hard to guess. Merely turn back the pages of time to the afternoon of October 6. That marked the real beginning of the Spankit's celebrated career. On that day he was transformed into the Bridal Car. The other vehicles had not opportunity to reach that high. And the next day the Spankit became the Honeymoon Car—the Double Honeymoon Car. And his career was made. If the Spankit does nothing else during the remainder of his career, he need not worry. He has played his part and played it nobly— the most famous of all the King's cars. This King doesn't happen to have any horses!

4

Benny Goodlow's Editorials

WHILE THE NEWS ITEMS AND LOCAL STORIES captured the interest of all readers, it was probably Benny's editorials that revealed his keen insight into the needs and problems of the church family.

A news item in one issue wrote of the illness of a member:

> She has been very brave and courageous. Sometimes she has been very low, but she would rally and come back again. We have often admired her gameness. We hope that she will be more than successful in this fight to regain her health. We cannot recommend a better place for her in her illness than the institution which she has selected. But to the care of trained nurses and able physicians must be added the mercy and help of our Lord who is able to do all things. The Lord can heal. With Him is the power to heal utterly, and He is a prayer-answering God. Let us rely on Him!

Illnesses and possibly deaths may have been the occasion that caused Benny to write this next editorial.

Strive to Be Ready

Psalm 48:1: "Great is the LORD, and greatly to be praised in the city of our God, in the mountain of his holiness."

No man knows when death will swoop down upon him. When a man rises in the morning, to go to his work, he does not know if he shall live to see sundown. He does not know when he leaves his door whether he will ever see his loved ones again. Life in this world is uncertain. There is no way to tell when it will end. It may end suddenly and with violence. Again it may endure for years and years. We do not know.

There are so many accidents. Hourly we have accidents. They occur to all classes and races of people. None are exempt. And so long as we have accidents, so long will the death toll continue. It used to be thought that if a young person possessed rugged health and strong and vigorous constitution, that he had many years of life before him. But we must reckon with accidents, the scourge of human existence. The strong and healthy may be proof against disease, but they are not proof against accidents. A strong man may be able to resist a contagious ailment, but his strength will not stand him in stead when he meets with accident. Accident is one of the things that makes life so insecure.

Every day we read in the papers about airplane crackups and automobile smashes and train wrecks and sinking ships and burning buildings, and hundreds of other mishaps, that take their toll of human life in an instant of time. There is nothing much that man can do about it. And accidents, being no respecter of persons, happen to the good as well as the bad. Therefore, it behooves every man to be ready. By being ready we mean ready to die. Ready to meet the Saviour.

So many men die suddenly, unexpectedly, who do not know Jesus. It is appalling the number of persons who die without Him. With life so uncertain, with tragic accidents so certain, a man should prepare himself. He should have Christ in his heart. He should believe in Jesus, that he might be assured of eternal life after work in earth is done.

Jesus is the only remedy. He is the balm in Gilead. He is the Answer. Seek ye the Lord while He may be found! For the greatest hope that can possibly live in the human heart is the great hope of glory, and this comes through Jesus Christ our Lord.

Benny Goodlow loved and supported his church. Never once did he print anything that hinted a criticism of his church, his pastor, or any of his fellow members. Sometimes his concern for the church, or for a situation he sensed was developing within the body that could cause harm, would produce an editorial that addressed the need in spiritual terms without pointing the finger at individuals.

His concern for the church to grow, which he expressed in one issue, may have prompted his longer editorial on "Prayer." In his first comment Benny said:

> All of us are heavily burdened for the church and desire to see it builded up. We want to see it grow and expand and become a factor in this community. We want to see new members come in. We know and believe in the power of prayer. We know that God can send us new members, and we know that He will if we pray to Him, for He is a prayer-answering God.

Later, he wrote a longer editorial that preached an eloquent sermon on the need for prayer in the life of every Christian:

Prayer!

> Hebrews 11:1: "Now faith is the substance of things hoped for, the evidence of things not seen."
>
> Faith, we see, is the substance of things hoped for and the evidence of things not seen, as the author of Hebrews tells us. Which means that if we believe in the Christ, whom we have not seen, if we believe in Him absolutely, without the least shadow of a doubt, then we have faith in Him. And if we have such faith in Him, it truly follows that we will worship Him, and will make our prayers to Him. If we have such faith, we will believe that He is our Advocate, our Intercessor, the One who stands be-

tween the Father and us, pleading our cause. And having this belief, there is no power that will prevent us from coming to Him in prayer.

God, our heavenly Father, created this vast and boundless universe, and all that it contains. Everything was made by God and His mighty power. He created the earth and put man upon it. He created the earth for His own pleasure, and it pleased Him to make man. He created man an intelligent and an upright creature, and it was His desire that man should worship Him. Sin, however, crept in, and man became a contrary creature, choosing the ways of unrighteousness, and for a time it seems that God's great plan has been interrupted; but the interruption is merely temporal, and this earth shall be as God first intended it, a righteous and holy habitation peopled by a righteous and holy race of intelligent beings who will worship and praise Him throughout eternity.

And we can attain to that righteous and holy world if we live our lives by faith, and concentrate upon our prayer life. For without prayer all is failure. Without prayer, souls cannot be saved nor can the church endure. Prayer is our test of faith. If we have faith, we will pray. If we have faith, we will believe that He is a prayer-answering God, and nothing in the world will keep us from coming to Him in secret to praise and worship Him.

Prayer is the golden chain which links us with Him. Prayer is the only connection we have with the Divine. And if we do not remain steadfast in our prayer life, our Christian experience will surely suffer. Indeed, we cannot have a Christian experience without prayer. It is said, and rightly so, that where there is no vision the people perish. And where there is no prayer there is no vision. If a man believes in God, he will pray. If a man believes in Christ, that He is our Saviour and Redeemer, that man will pray. Prayer is the test of our faith. If we believe, we will pray. If we do not believe, we will not pray. Faith is the substance of the things hoped for. We pray because we hope. Because hope springs eternally in the human breast, as the poet says, we continue to pray. And this hope is based on faith. Continue ye steadfast in prayer!

Benny Goodlow viewed his beloved church with a keenly sensitive spirit. He loved us all, and if he sensed any one of us was beginning to stray or was being tempted to set his own will up in opposition to the will of God, an editorial like "The Contrary Spirit" was sure to appear in an early issue of the *Bulletin.*

The Contrary Spirit

1 Samuel 13:9: "And Saul said, Bring hither a burnt offering to me, and peace offerings. And he offered the burnt offering."

Many, many sermons have been preached about King Saul, the first ruler of united Israel. He has been held up as the highest expression of self-will and stubbornness. He has been held up as a more disobedient servant than Adam. Saul was given a kingdom and a people. He was given the divine right to rule and reign. He was highly favored in every way. He was certainly fitted to be a king. He was a kingly figure. He stood head and shoulders above any of his subjects.

And it cannot be said that in his youth, Saul was not a worthy man. The first picture we get of him, as he goes in search of his father's sheep which had gone astray, impresses us with his likelihood. When he confers with the judge and prophet Samuel, we are struck with his humbleness. It is even said that a new heart was given him and that he became a different man. This meant that he was properly fitted at that time to be king. In later years, David always referred to King Saul as the Lord's anointed.

But as the years travel on, we get a different picture of this monarch who started out so auspiciously. Success had probably gone to his head, and he became proud and vain and austere and self-reliant. He departed from God who had been his Mainstay. He did things as he wanted to do them and not as they should have been done. He became contrary.

First Samuel 13:9, which reads, "And Saul said, Bring hither a burnt offering to me, and peace offerings. And he offered the burnt offering," relates how he offered a burnt offering when he should have waited until Samuel arrived. The place was at Gilgal. Israel was about to go to battle with their ancient and traditional enemies, the Philistines. But Israel was in a strait and sore afraid. Many of them hid in rocks and caves. After Saul offered the burnt offering, Samuel came and upbraided him. Saul, naturally, offered alibis which were not acceptable. Samuel told him plainly that he had not kept the Lord's command, and that the Lord had rejected him from being king, having found a more worthy man than he to fill that position.

Another incident in the life of Saul, which has formed the basis for countless sermons, is his adventure with the Amalekites. He had been instructed by the Lord to make a full end of them, sparing none, not even the women and children and sucking babes.

The sacred record says that "Saul smote the Amalekites from Havilah until thou comest to Shur, that is over against Egypt. And he took Agag the king of the Amalekites alive, and utterly destroyed all the people with the edge of the sword" (1 Samuel 15:7 and 8).

But even after putting on this great battle, and destroying the Amalekites with a great slaughter, Saul did not wholly walk in the commandment of the Lord. He kept Agag alive, and salvaged cattle and sheep "not a little."

So we see the contrary spirit in Saul, which clung to him to the end of his days. His last act before Gilboa was to confer with a witch who had a "familiar" spirit, contrary to the law of God.

As a total end to his kingly career, Saul filled a suicide's grave. What a terrible tragedy his life had become, and all because of that harsh and tyrannical contrary spirit that he nurtured in his heart. It was an awful price for him to pay when it could have been so different.

Beware of the contrary spirit. Let it not engulf nor enslave you. Do not force that noble soul of yours to bow to that little narrow, contrary will. Willpower may be an asset—but crass stubbornness is so often mistaken for willpower. When one uses his or her will to disobey the commandments of God, then willpower ceases to be an asset. It becomes a curse.

Beware of the contrary spirit.

5

An Unforgettable Era Comes to an End

THE YEARS WENT BY. Eventually Benny's mother passed away, and not long afterward, Lily also died. The whole congregation mourned their loss and crowded the little church to share their funeral services. Benny and his sister Katy continued to be an integral part of the church family, more closely knit together than ever by our common loss.

Then a wonderful thing happened to Benny. The government announced that a bonus would be given to each veteran who had served in World War I. This meant Benny would receive a check for several hundred dollars. This would be comparable to several thousand dollars today. Everyone rejoiced with him. The first thing he did after receiving that bonus check was to purchase a brand-new typewriter. He gave his old one to my father, who used it for many years.

The bonus was a mixed blessing for Benny. He loved ice cream. He never seemed to get enough of it. Now he could afford it. It was not unusual for him to show up at the back door of the church parsonage with ingredients for the "Shepherdess" to put together so that he and the Shepherd could churn homemade ice cream. Sometimes he would show up with store-bought ice cream, and an instant party would take place.

But Benny was a diabetic. The ice cream contributed to deterioration of his health. When he learned he would have to have a leg amputated, somehow we all knew it wouldn't be long before Benny would be leaving us, and it wasn't. Probably today's medical science would have prolonged his life. But October 4, 1936, Benny slipped away to heaven from his hospital bed. He was only 46 years old.

His passing left a big gap in that little congregation, for we lost not only Benny but his *Bulletin* as well. His weekly publication was so unique and it represented such devotion that it was impossible for anyone to duplicate his work.

Katy was the last of the Goodlow family. She was in many ways opposite to her brother, but what a precious person she was. If my parents left town, my sister and I would be sent to stay with Katy. Acts of kindness she repeated proved her love for us and our family. One of my vivid recollections is of an occasion when it seemed as though the depression had caught up with us in all its stark reality. There wasn't a single bit of food left in our house to eat, and we had gone to bed hungry. I recall crying myself to sleep, wondering when we would have food again. Later that same night my parents awakened me. They took me to the dining room where a basket of sandwiches and other food was waiting to be shared. Katy had been there, they said, and brought the food to us. Is it any wonder this woman, who barely had enough to eat herself, had a special place in our hearts?

Katy experienced some dark days. As the last surviving member of her family she now was her own sole provider. She had been working in the sewing room set up by President Roosevelt's Works Progress Administration program. That specific project was completed, and she and others were laid off. Unless the town could get another sewing project approved by the WPA, there was no other job to be had.

Resourceful as Katy was, she decided to serve meals in her home. Unfortunately her entrepreneurial attempts were unsuccessful, and she decided she would have to move to a larger city. When Katy left, it was as sad for us as the funeral of her family members had been.

Katy returned only once, for a visit of a few hours. She and my mother sat in our car for a long, long time catching up on the latest in each other's lives. They were in the car, for in our small parsonage there was no quiet corner where they could be alone to enjoy the "girl talk" that they claimed as their own. Such was their friendship, and such is my memory of four precious people who made a profound impact on my young life.

6

Musings

IT HAS BEEN ABOUT 60 YEARS since Benny published the *Bulletin.* Inquiries made to those who were part of that fellowship have turned up a number of issues. The paper is yellowed with age and shows signs of deterioration. It is fortunate, perhaps even miraculous, that these copies have been kept. But the fact that they have testifies to how important these pages were in the lives of the people.

Perhaps there is a lesson for all of us in Benny and his *Bulletin.* In spite of our circumstances, and whatever our limitations may appear to be, we may accomplish what we desire to do if we put our minds to it. Benny did not become editor of a great city newspaper, as I'm sure he would like to have been. No one ever elected him as editor of a weekly church bulletin. He simply found a way to do it himself and brought joy and blessing to our small congregation for many years. I dare say no editor has left more lasting or more pleasant memories in the minds of his readers than those left by Benny in the minds of readers of the *Bulletin.* As an editor and a writer Benny was a shining success. He earned a respect not only for his happy, optimistic outlook but also for his ability to express himself on paper. Benny Goodlow deserves a place in history. He demonstrated how one can fill a niche—even one carved out for himself—and bless the lives of many. Perhaps even now there will be those who will read these pages and be inspired to fulfill their dreams.

I have had the privilege of traveling extensively to churches in the United States and have met with many believers from York, Nebraska. Very few now directly recall the events of those days, but the legends and the influences have carried over to the second and third generations. I have found not only faithfulness to spiritual roots but also membership in the same denomination as that little Nebraska church. Many of these people became successful business and professional people and are active in one form or another of their church. Benny Goodlow's *Bulletin* obviously provided some of the significant "spiritual glue" that produced this bonding.

Benny found in his job of washing dishes his means of becoming the editor he longed to be. As a child I loved and admired him greatly. Today I cherish his memory and take great joy and satisfaction in sharing it with others.

For those of us who were there and remember, each page of these yellowed copies of the *Bulletin* is a precious jewel out of the past. Most of what he wrote would not have meaning to those who weren't there. But once in a while Benny would editorialize with thoughts worth saving and sharing with a much larger audience. It seems fitting now to add some of those editorials here, in the hope that they will challenge and encourage readers today, as they did when Benny first wrote them, many years ago.

The Forgiving Father

Isaiah 1:18: "Come now, and let us reason together, saith the LORD: though your sins be as scarlet, they shall be as white as snow; though they be red like crimson, they shall be as wool."

The above word from the mighty pen of Isaiah is a most heartening text. It is a strong text, which assures us with a great assurance that God forgives. The fact that God forgives is the most wonderful piece of news ever broadcasted. If our God was not a forgiving God, all of the billions of people which have lived upon this earth since the Creation would be eternally lost. But God forgives! No matter what our sins may be, if we repent, He is faithful to forgive us our unrighteousness.

In His Holy Book it says that whatsoever measure you mete, it shall be measured to you again, which means that if you will forgive those who do evil against you, God will also forgive you your sins. But you cannot harbor ill will toward your neighbor and expect the blessings of God to descend upon you. In plain and unvarnished English, the way you treat people is the way God is going to treat you.

If you desire to benefit from this wonderful text, which was written by one of the greatest writers of all time, you must be willing to forgive others, as you, yourself, want to be forgiven.

In one of His discourses, Jesus admonishes us to do unto others as we would like for them to do unto us, and this great thought is in keeping with the policy of forgiveness. You must not expect blessings from the Father of Lights if you still have the old carnal spirit in your heart, which constrains you to hold grudges and harbor malice.

God wants to reason with you. God is most responsible. God is just and fair. He does nothing without an explanation. He wants to forgive you your sins, but you must meet certain conditions to obtain the blessings. Then it is that God washes you whiter than snow, no matter how crimson your sins may be.

❊ ❊ ❊

Falling Away. Why?

Genesis 2:22: "And the rib, which the LORD God had taken from man, made he a woman, and brought her unto the man."

There are many lives to live in this world. There are many roads open to every man and woman. There are many opportunities offered.

But all of these lives and these high roads and these opportunities are not worth choosing. There are lives that are lived that are absolutely profitless, and there are high roads that lead to certain and to-tal destruction, and there are opportunities that only open to the ambitious doors of crime.

On the other hand, there are lives that are lived that are pure and beautiful and transcendent. And there are high roads that lead to eternal bliss, and there are opportunities which offer to the seeker the privilege of serving Christ Jesus our Redeemer.

But so often when there are those who get this privilege to serve Jesus, they serve for a little while, and then fly away. They become offended and imagine that they are taking the wise course of repudiating the Master, but they are only bringing confusion upon their own heads.

Some, however, are inherently weak and succumb to the baleful temptations of the world and drift back to the useless things of life. These are they who desire to have Jesus and still hold on to some of the "pleasant" things of life. Once they have fallen away, it is a hard task to reclaim them.

But the most puzzling backslider of all is he or she who assumes a "mad" spell and quits the church to spite somebody. These carry their feelings and emotions on their sleeves, and the least little thing peeves them. They often wrongfully imagine that they have been slighted and immediately seek ways and means of getting even, which is totally unchristian. Or perhaps they imagine that some other member is being accorded more opportunities to sing specials or to hold office or to be entrusted with some desirable duty. Their envy and jealousy constrains them to "quit coming out." They think that by going into a "peeve" and assuming a stubborn and contrary attitude, they will gain their point. More often than not they lose more than they can ever hope to gain.

Indeed, we believe that the church member who falls away through envy or jealousy or spite or peevishness is much harder to bring back into the fold than the one who falls away through love of the world. The professing Christian who still has envy and hate and spite and pride in his or her heart is not better than an infidel. The professing Christian who grieves the Holy Spirit because the imagination suggests that he or she isn't getting the lion's share of the privileges and desires to work a spite against someone isn't any better than a hypocrite.

What to do with those who fall away so easily is one of the biggest problems the church has to deal with. We can understand the person who goes back to drinking or smoking or other worldly activities, but it is difficult to understand the person who backslides through envy and spite and jealousy.

❊ ❊ ❊

The Cry That Goes Up!

Psalm 40:1: "I waited patiently for the LORD; and he inclined unto me, and heard my cry."

It is true that the Lord will hear our distressful cry in the midst of our trials and troubles. He is not slack concerning His promises as some count slackness. He is ever ready to help us in the time of need. Every Christian upon the face of the earth this day can testify to that. He hears and He answers prayers. Even we, who believe, would be a bit surprised if we but knew the thousands of prayers which are answered daily. But we do not hear about these thousands and thousands of prayers which have been answered, simply because the world does not talk about the works of God like they do the works of man. Let a man accomplish a feat of some kind, like flying across the ocean in a plane, or writing a popular book, and the whole world goes into spasm in the effort to make a hero of him. But let Christ save a wicked and wretched soul from hell, and transform that wicked soul into the soul of a saint, which is the greatest possible achievement that can be wrought, and the newspapers and magazines and periodicals are silent. Only in the testimony meeting, where true Christians gather to worship, is the work of Christ recognized and praised.

Yet, Jesus patiently strives with the hearts of people and continues to offer them this one and only way of escape from the wrath to come. Even today, in this enlightened age, He is scoffed at and derided and mocked and insulted with the multitudes crying out in favor of Barabbas, against the Son of God. But in spite of the world's hate of Him, He is still faithful and true. He still inclines His ear toward us to hear our cry of distress. Even those who hate Him and do all manner of despite toward Him can receive of the blessing if they but repent and believe. No other Being but Christ in God could be so patient with humanity. No other Being could forgive as readily as He. We cry unto Him and He hears. He not only hears but He answers. That is the manner of God we worship. We give Him thanks.

✳ ✳ ✳

Argumentation

Luke 8:21: "And he answered and said unto them, My mother and my brethren are these which hear the word of God, and do it."

There is not much that can be said in favor of argumentation. Plain, bullheaded argument settles nothing, for the simple reason that the arguer doesn't want to settle anything.

The chronic arguer is only intent upon impressing his opponent with his own vast knowledge of things and his own glorified wisdom and learning. The subject of discussion doesn't matter so much to the chronic arguer just so long as he has sufficient knowledge of it to remain in the conversation and display his arrogance and stubbornness.

Argument never leads to conviction but usually results in feelings that are not pleasant. No one delights in having some long-winded person inform them that they don't know much, and no one takes delight in being literally forced to accept somebody else's opinions and ideas, which the chronic arguer wants you to do.

But wait a minute. There is such a thing as intelligent discussion against which there is no law. Two or more persons can indulge in a sane and sensible discussion and thresh out a subject or a theme along the line of reason. Intelligent discussion is helpful, educational, and oftentimes inspiring; and there is not a more enjoyable experience than to contact somebody with whom you can talk upon the themes and subject which are nearest and dearest to your heart.

There is another form of vocal exercise which is not condemnable. This is the amusement which one derives out of an argument "just for fun." Generally it takes the form of teasing, and such arguments, if they can be called that, occur more frequently between men and women. They are carried on in fun and never leave rancor or bitterness in the heart. The person who indulges in fun arguments must possess a broad sense of humor.

✳ ✳ ✳

Knowledge

Proverbs 1:7: "The fear of the LORD is the beginning of knowledge: but fools despise wisdom and instruction."

All true civilization is based upon our knowledge of the Lord. Where God is not known, there is no true civilization. We, in this generation, are wiser in many things than our predecessors were, because we know more about God. We have advanced far and are still advancing, making new discoveries, bringing to light strange and unknown things, and all because we know the Lord.

But some people will scoff at that thought and say that man has advanced because of his own strength and his own individual efforts, and point to the Mazda lamp and the telephone and the locomotive and the automobile and the radio and the airplane and the telegraph, as proofs of man's ability to make his own world; but these instruments and inventions and discoveries add nothing to man's spiritual progress. They make for comfort, convenience, and enjoyment, but pagans are capable of making the same discoveries and inventions. Machines and motors are not the hallmark of Christian civilization.

Man, however, is not alone responsible for the many great inventions that we have. Man can do nothing without God, who permitted man to make these discoveries, and it was God who taught man how to dig into the earth to bring forth the treasures hidden there.

Radio is not the result of man's wisdom. Radio is a creation of God. It was God who placed the Hertzian waves in the atmosphere, which makes radio communication possible. It was God who showed man how to bring forth the incandescent lamp, which is so highly commended. Men give all the glory to man for this invention, but He who created the sun would have no trouble in teaching an intelligent creature how to form an electric lamp. And the same reasoning can be applied to the airplane. The wing is the instrument used in flying. All creatures that fly have wings. And it was God who created the wing. Therefore, man got his idea of the airplane from *Him*.

The fact of the matter is, all of man's ideas came from God. All the inventions that we have in the world are designed after something which God has made. The submarine duplicates the whale. The tank, which is used in war, reminds one of the elephant. Airplanes are copies of birds and insects. The telephone is akin to the ear. Huge buildings are erected after the principles of the human anatomy. The motor engine is man's nearest approach to the human heart. And one can go on down the line and see on every hand where man has copied the works of God, which proves, conclusively, that man can do nothing without God.

7

Reflections

THE OCTOBER 22, 1935, copy of the *Bulletin* is particularly noteworthy for revealing Benny's zest for life and the fun he had in writing about people. Much of this issue has to do with one of the young couples returning from their honeymoon. Apparently relatives of the bride and groom had accompanied them on their wedding trip—justification for much editorializing on the subject. (The bride, now widowed and 80 years of age, located this issue among her own keepsakes and has shared it.)

It is also interesting to note that Benny, age 45 when writing this issue, spoke of himself as an old "fogy," poking fun at himself as well as others. Referring to an upcoming event being planned by the young people of the church for the young people, Benny wrote:

> The young people are now making great preparations for an elaborate entertainment on the evening of the 30th of October. They are even planning on out of town guests. But only the young people will attend. We who are ancient and doddering and fogy will not be included. So why don't we old fogies give a party of some kind? We do not mean a Halloween party. We do not like the idea of Halloween parties. But we could give an old fogy party some time, and just sit around and drink tea and talk about our ailments.

The ability he possessed not to take himself too seriously persists in this 1935 issue. Writing of a prayer meeting that took place in the home of one of the members, he said:

> The prayer meeting was wonderful, and the leader brought us a helpful message, and the testi-

monies were good. It was after he had given his testimony that the Editor nearly spoiled everything by imagining that there was one more chair in the row than there was. He made an attempt to sit on the chair that was missing, but the atmosphere was not substantial enough to support his Fat Duck weight, so he was precipitated to the floor to the high amusement of those present.

But it was humor at its best when he described a wedding that had taken place in the church. He wrote in what he called the language of Ol' Man River:

"To me," sez he, rubbing capable fingers through his shaggy hair, "as they stood up there 'midst them flow'rs an' things, a-starin' at the preacher man wide-eyed, they seemed jes' like a bunch o' scared children 'bout tuh give a program they hadn't practised!"

In collecting materials for this book, I found myself emotionally stirred in finding one of the last editorials Benny had written. That he was inspired as he wrote, one cannot question. That God already was giving him glimpses of the future that undoubtedly had great meaning for him, I'm confident.

Look to the Promises

Matthew 24:35: "Heaven and earth shall pass away, but my words shall not pass away."

There never lived a being upon the earth who could positively state that his words would not, in the course of time, pass away, saving Jesus Christ. He alone of all the billions who have inhabited this planet is able to sustain the words He uttered during His earthly ministry. The Word He was referring to is the Bible. The Bible is God's Word. The Bible contains the truth of God. In it is all the knowledge and truth of the Divine that has ever been revealed to humanity. There is no other source from which this beautiful and redeeming truth can be drawn.

And upon this Truth, the Promises are based. If there was no Bible, there would be no promises.

Jesus promised, just before He was to depart from this earth, that He was going to prepare a wonderful *home* for us, that where He was, there we may be also. We believe that it is a *city*, a city of gold and precious stones, of castles and palaces and mansions, such as this world never saw. We believe that it is a land of eternal bliss and peace and joy, where we shall obtain everything that shall make us indescribably happy. We believe that in that land we shall remain young forever—eternal youth—and that we shall be the possessors of strong and vigorous and wholesome and rugged bodies, bodies that shall never grow tired, that shall never know exhaustion, that shall never wax feeble.

The promises of God, made sure to us through Jesus Christ our Lord! They are worth waiting for. Yea, they are worth suffering for. Selah!

* * *

In less than a year, Benny Goodlow took up residence in the city of gold.